Thank you for purchasing my book. Your patronage is much appreciated. I hope the book brings some joy and entertainment.

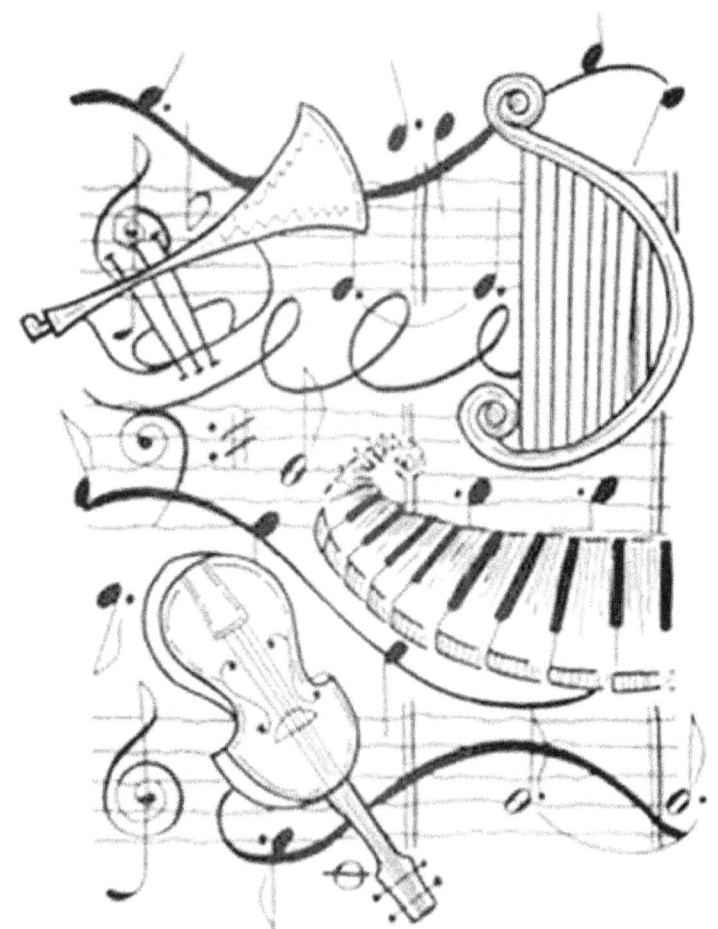

This Book Belongs To

_____

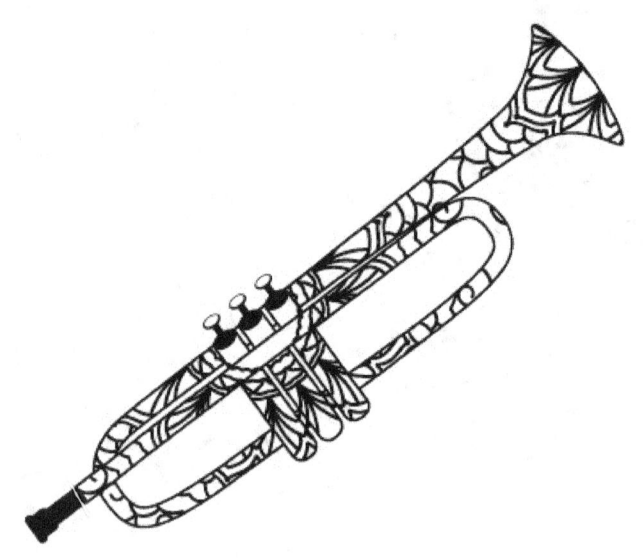

"Music does more than soothe the soul, it brings balance to the mind, body, and soul."
Beatrice Berry

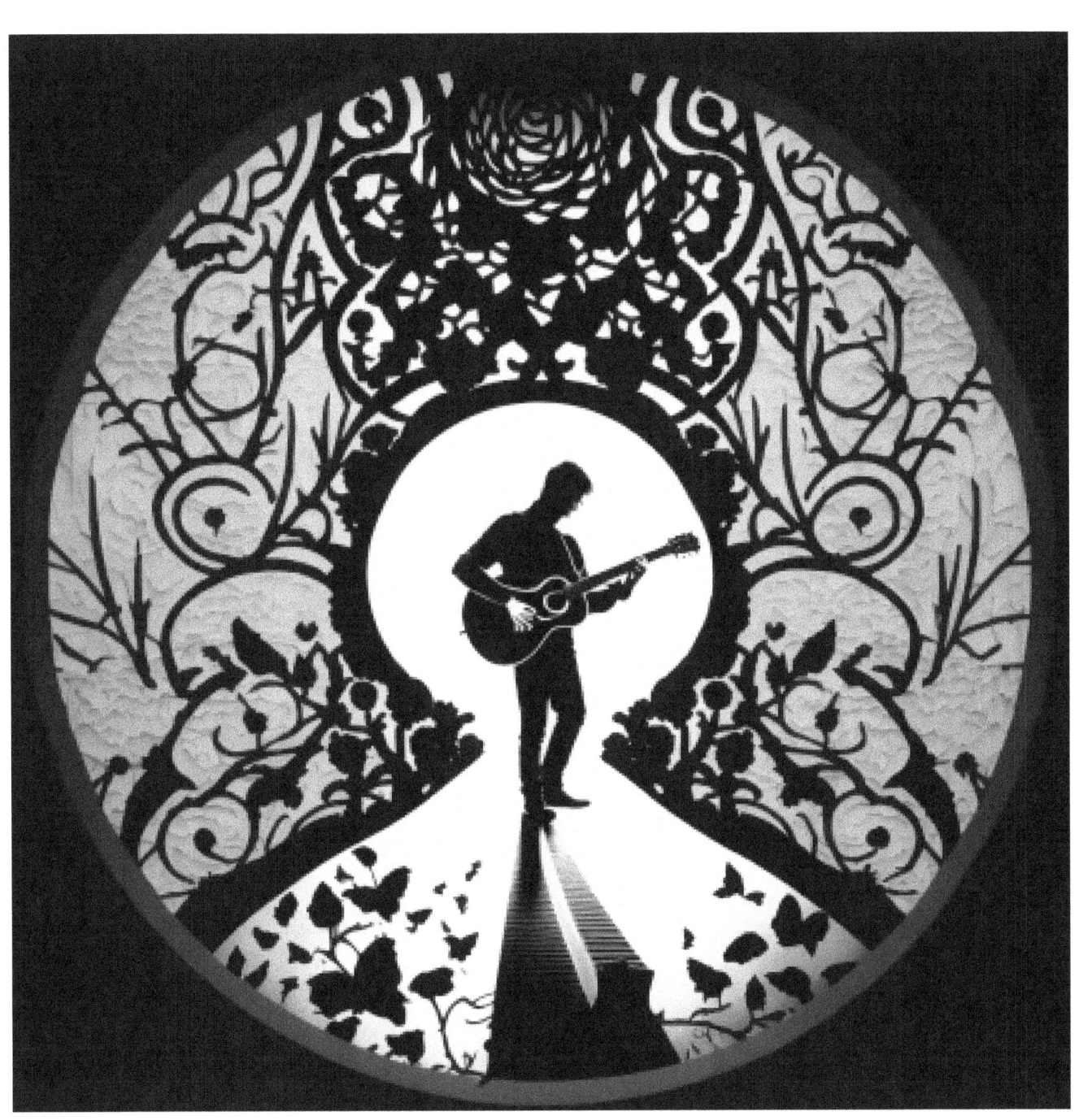

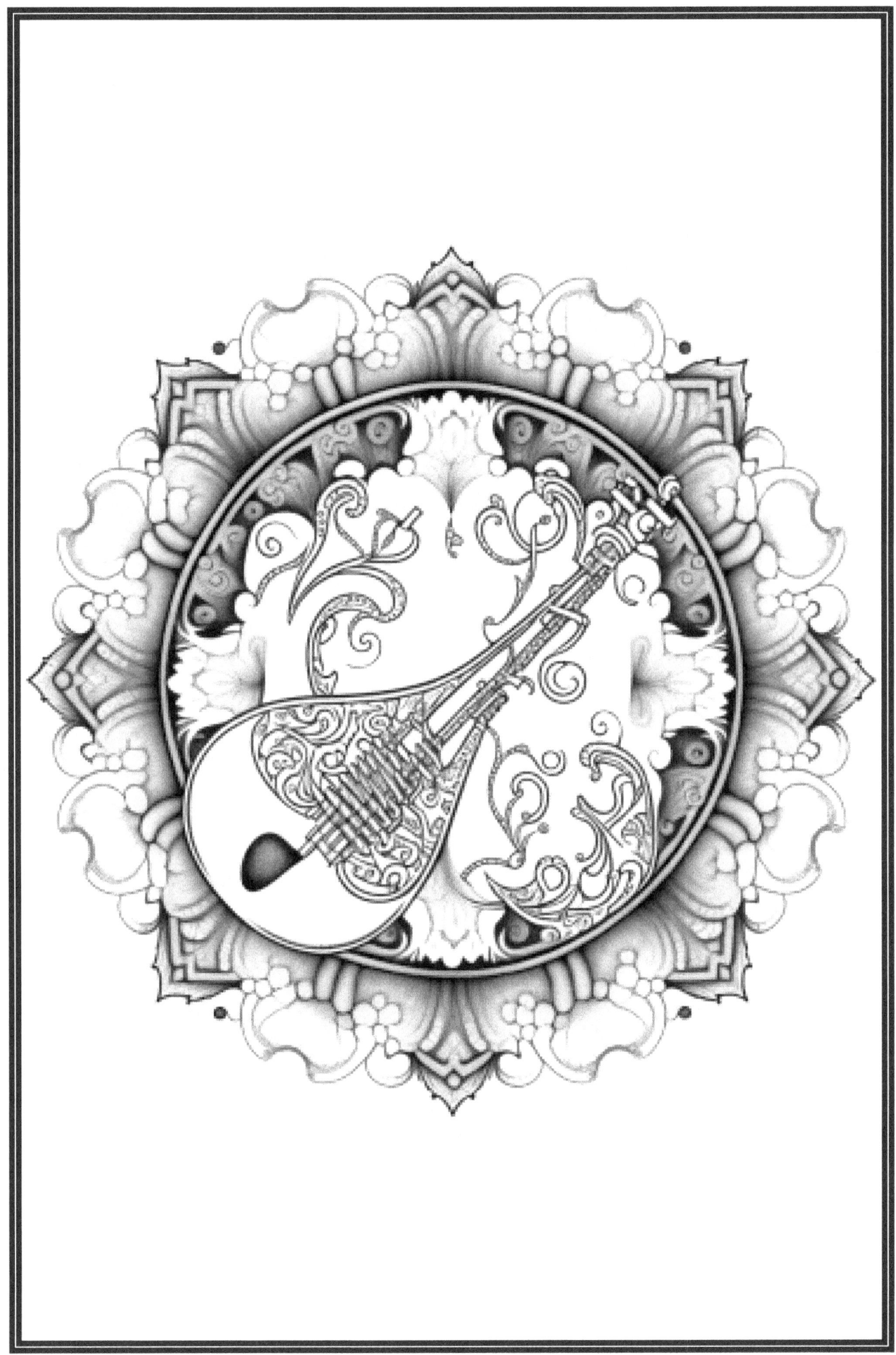

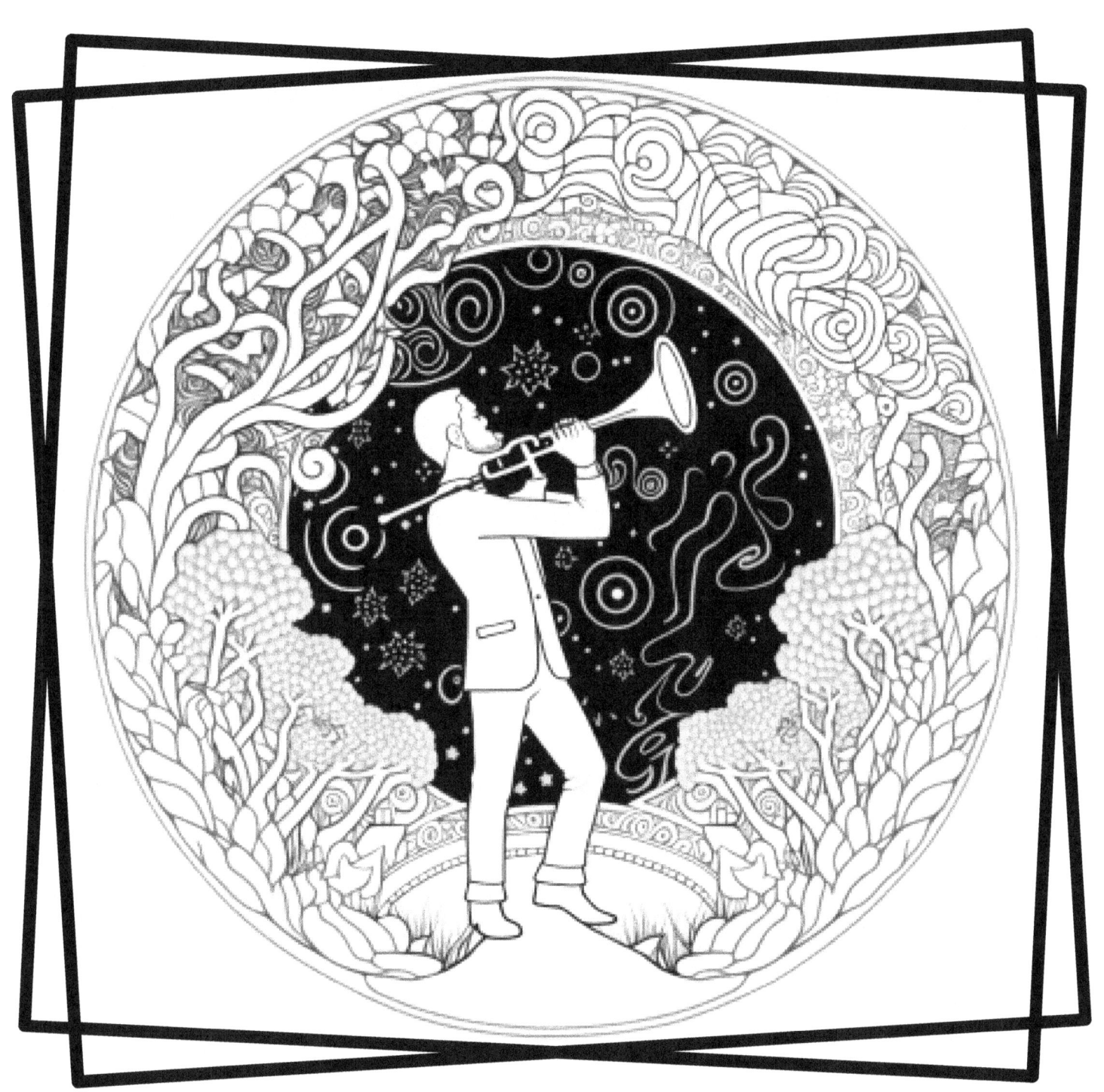

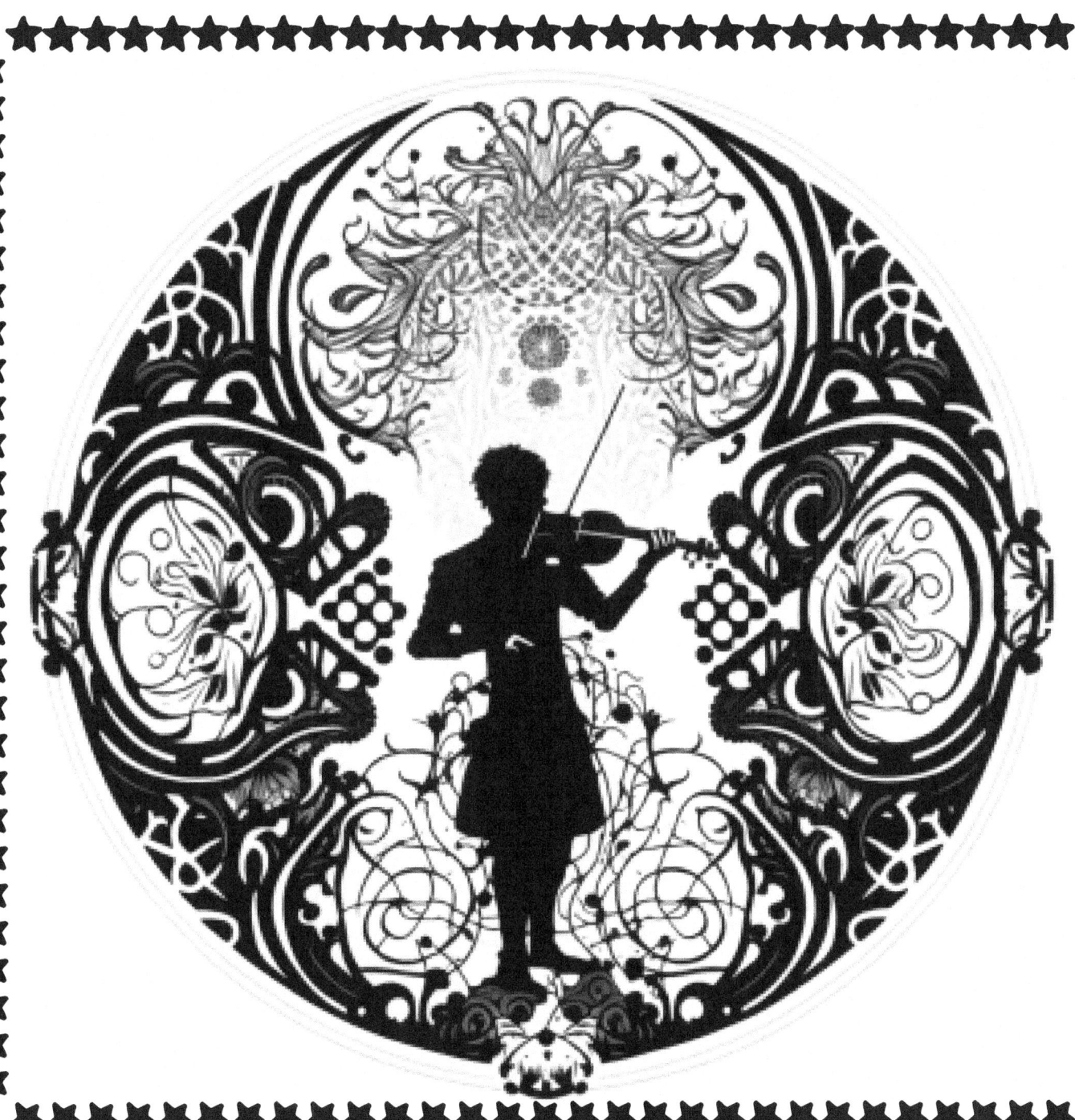

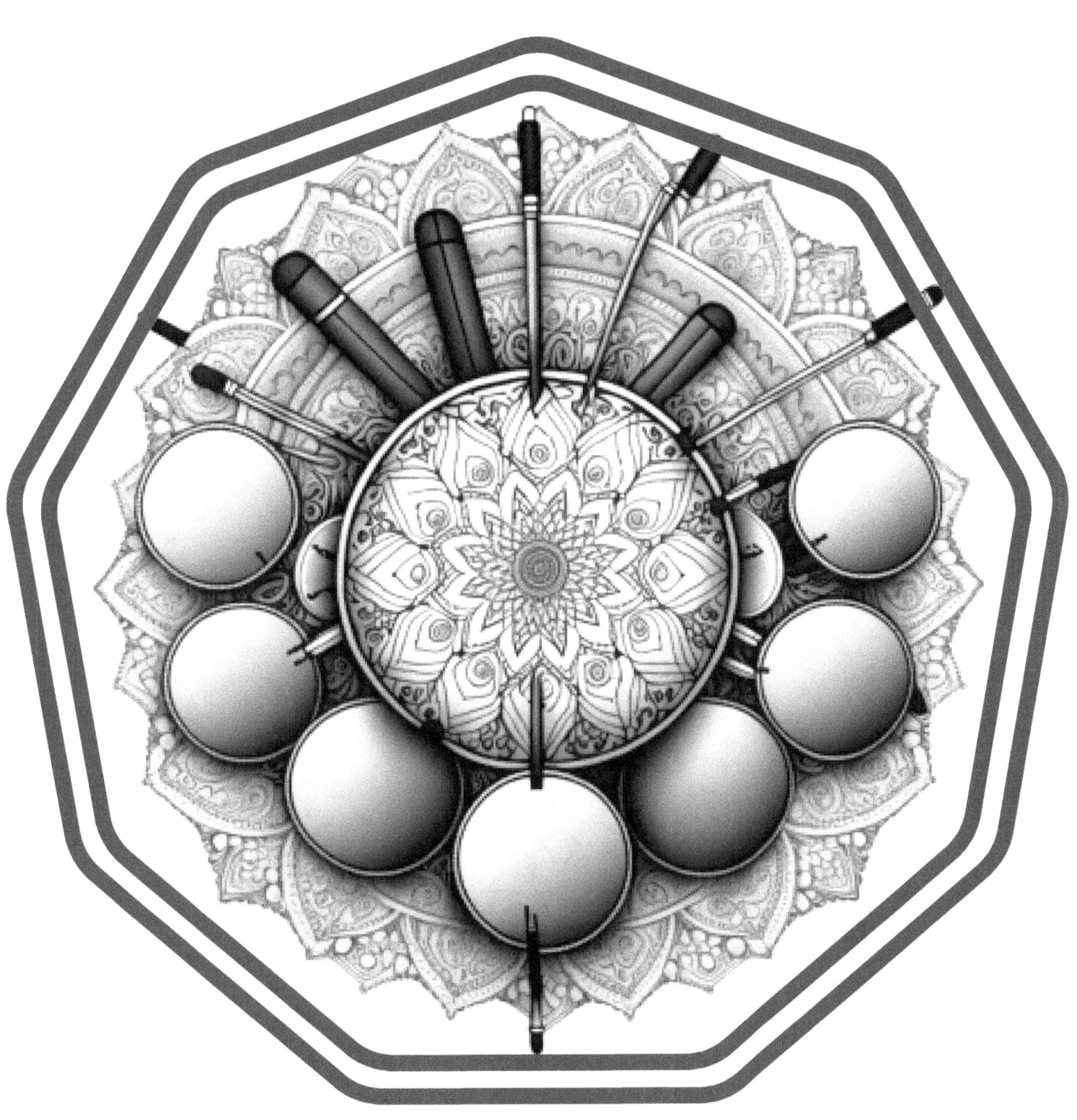

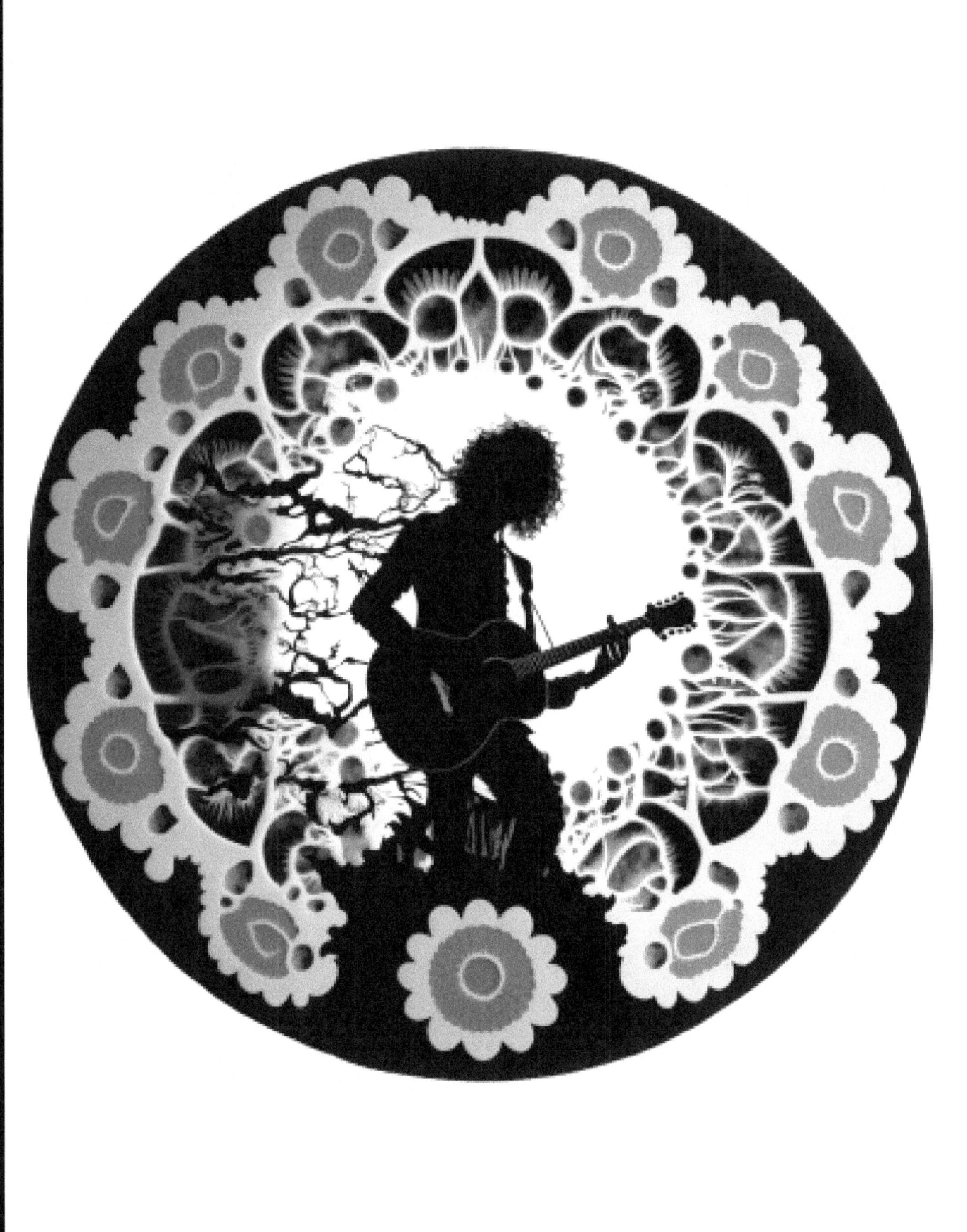

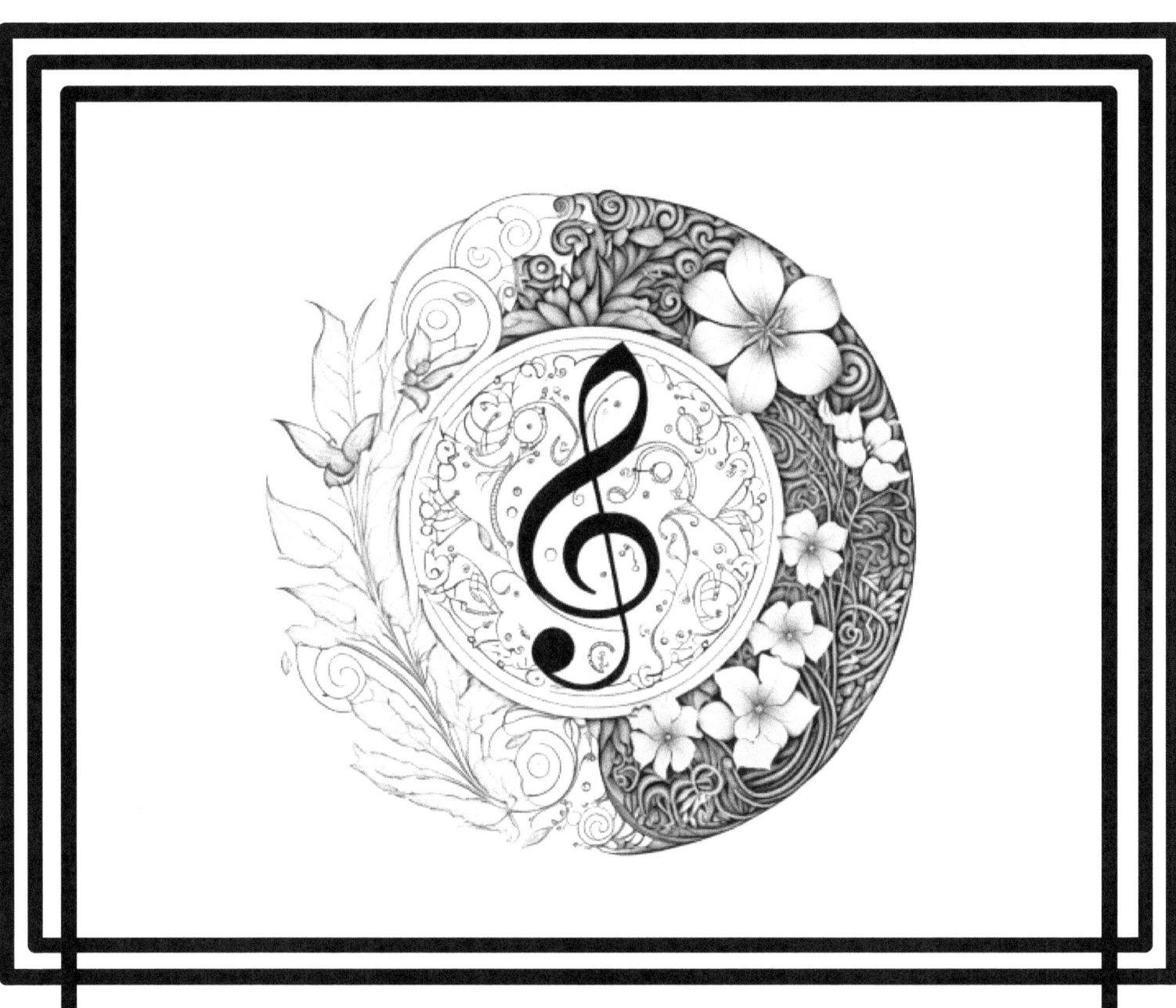

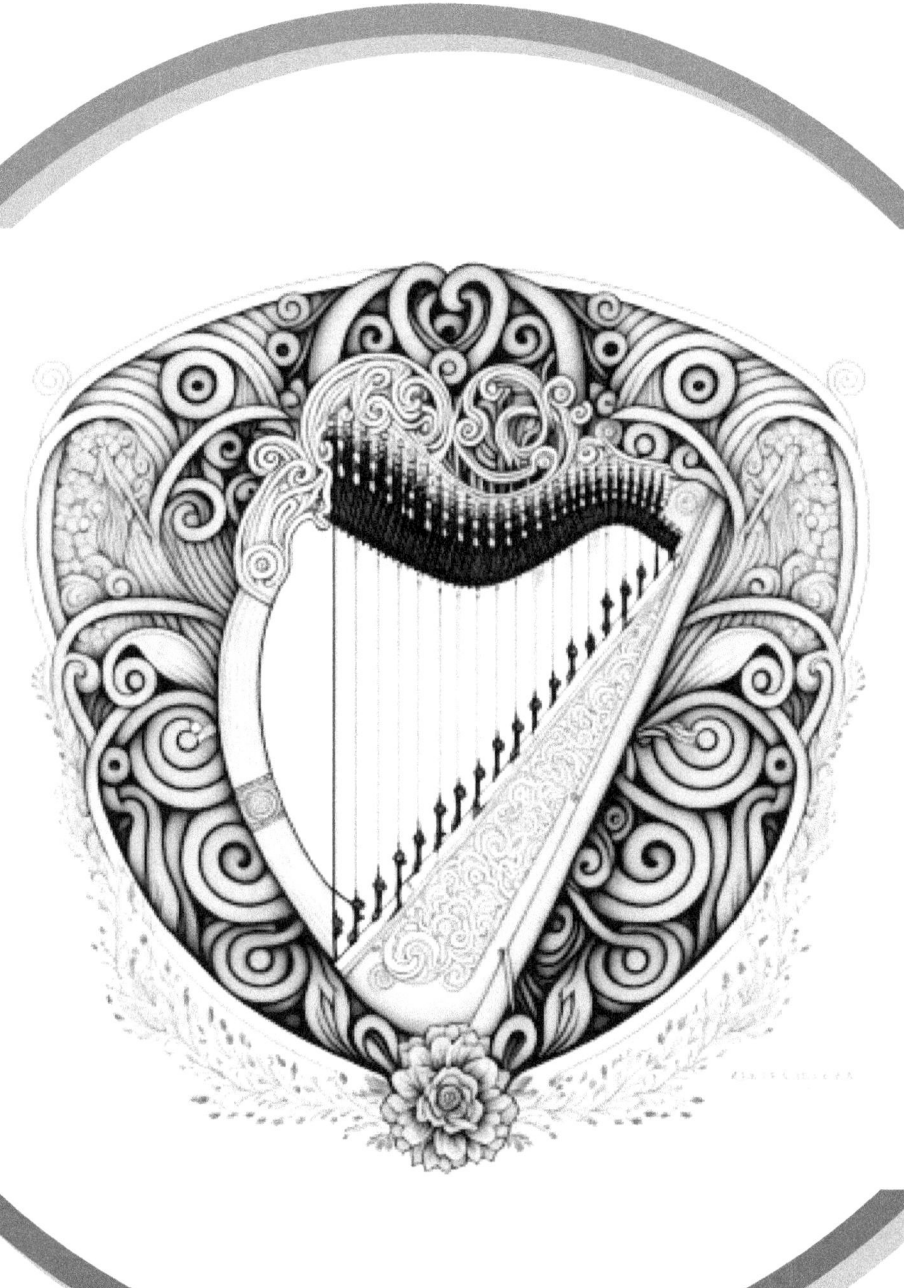

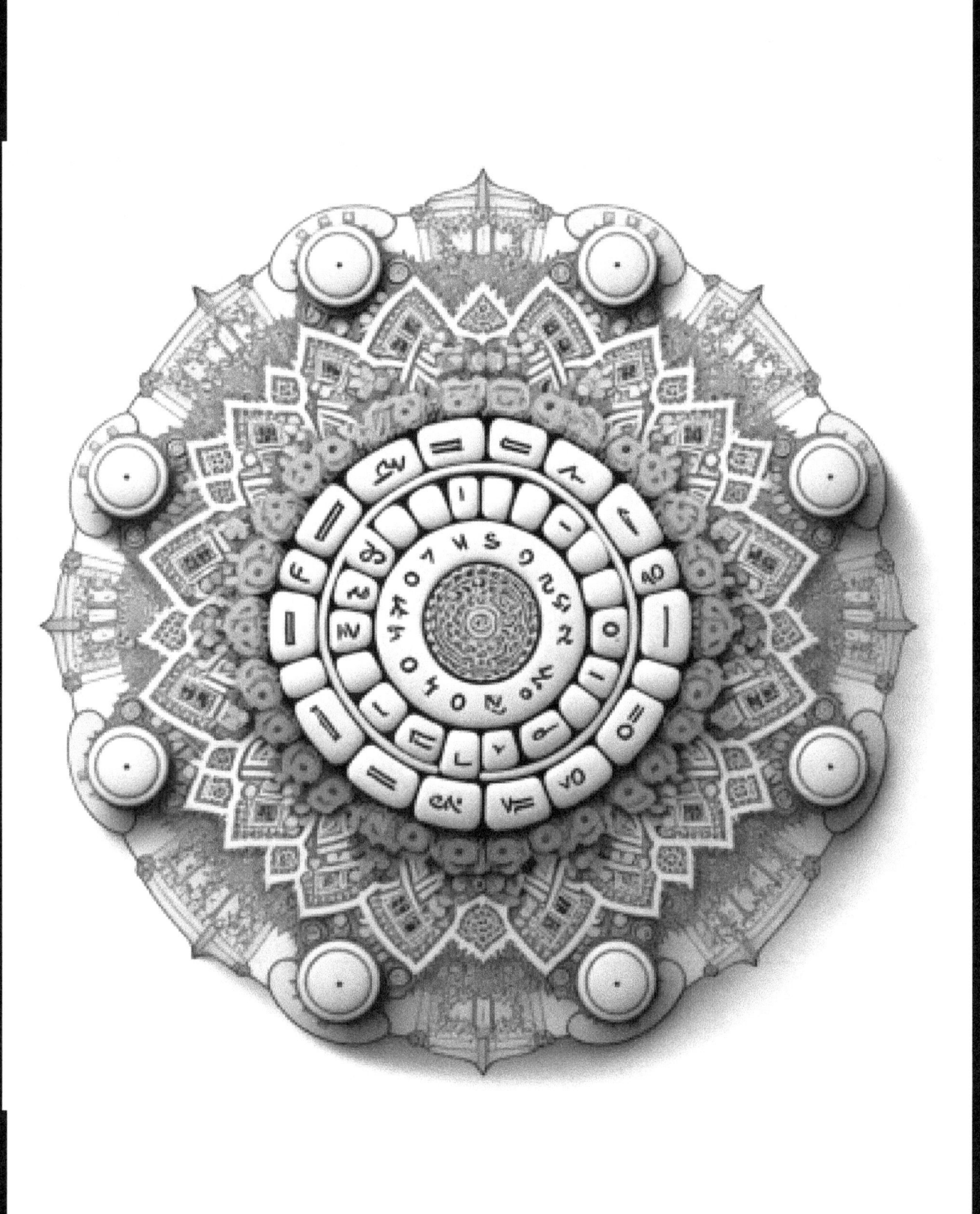

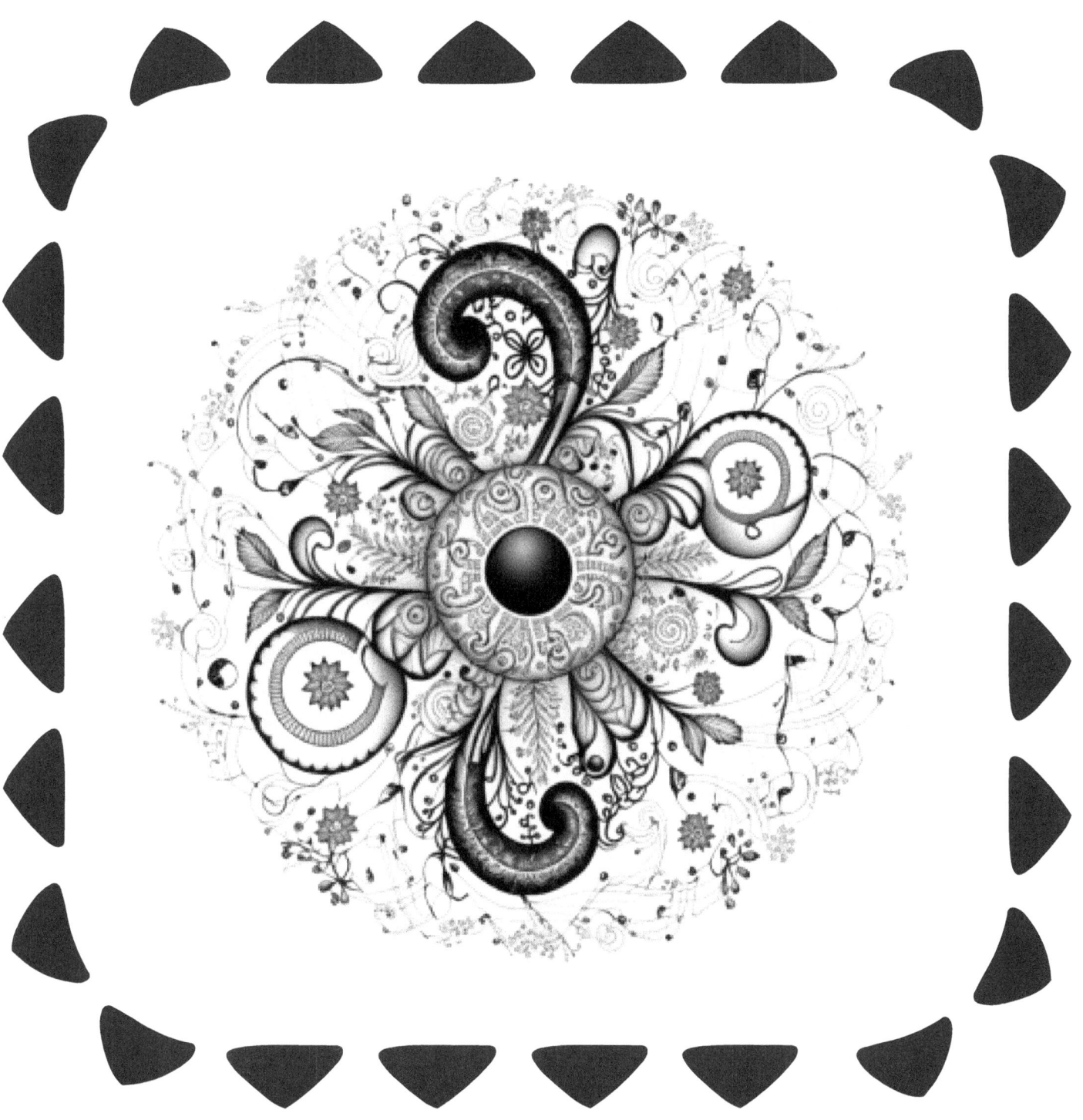

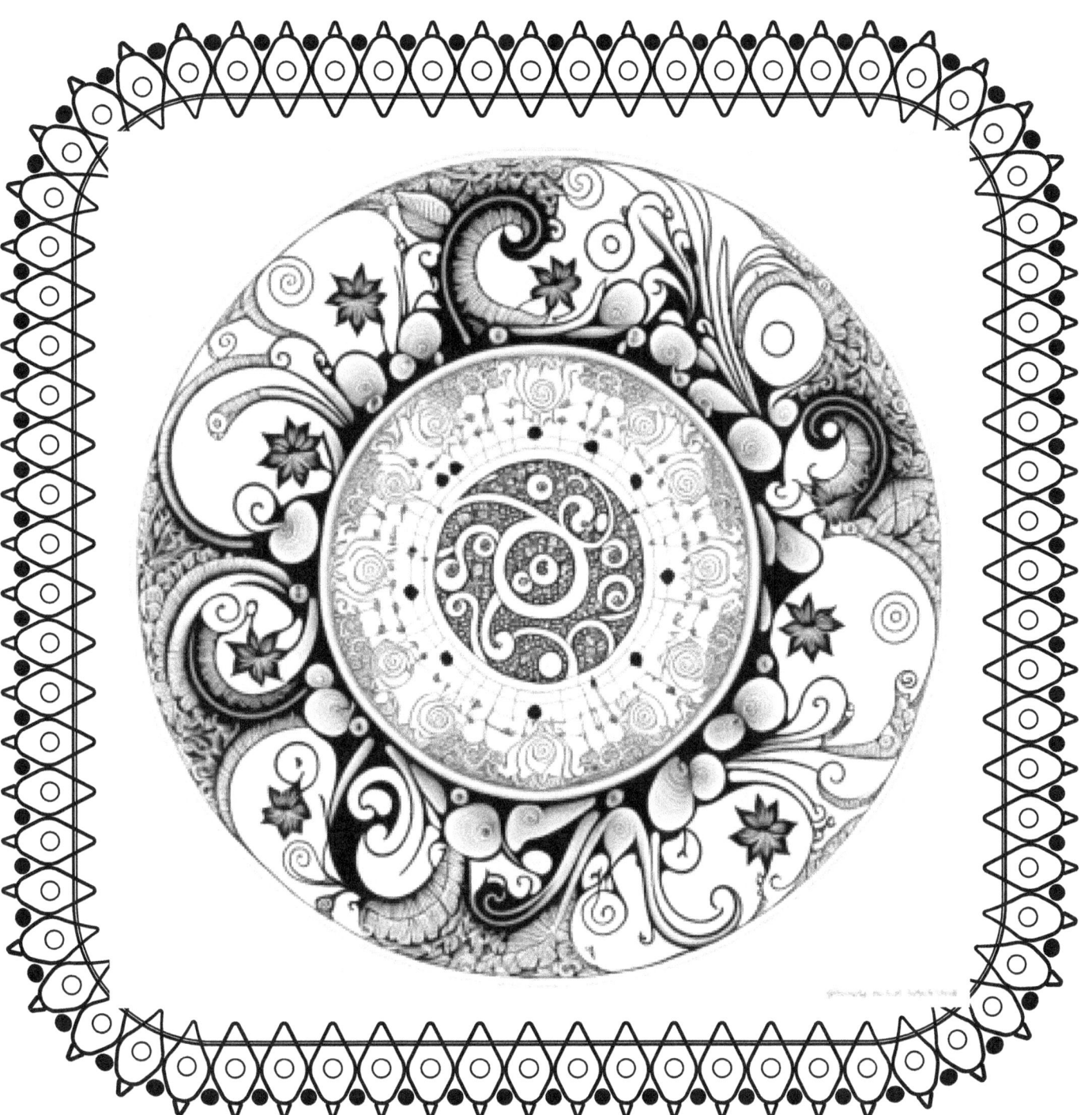

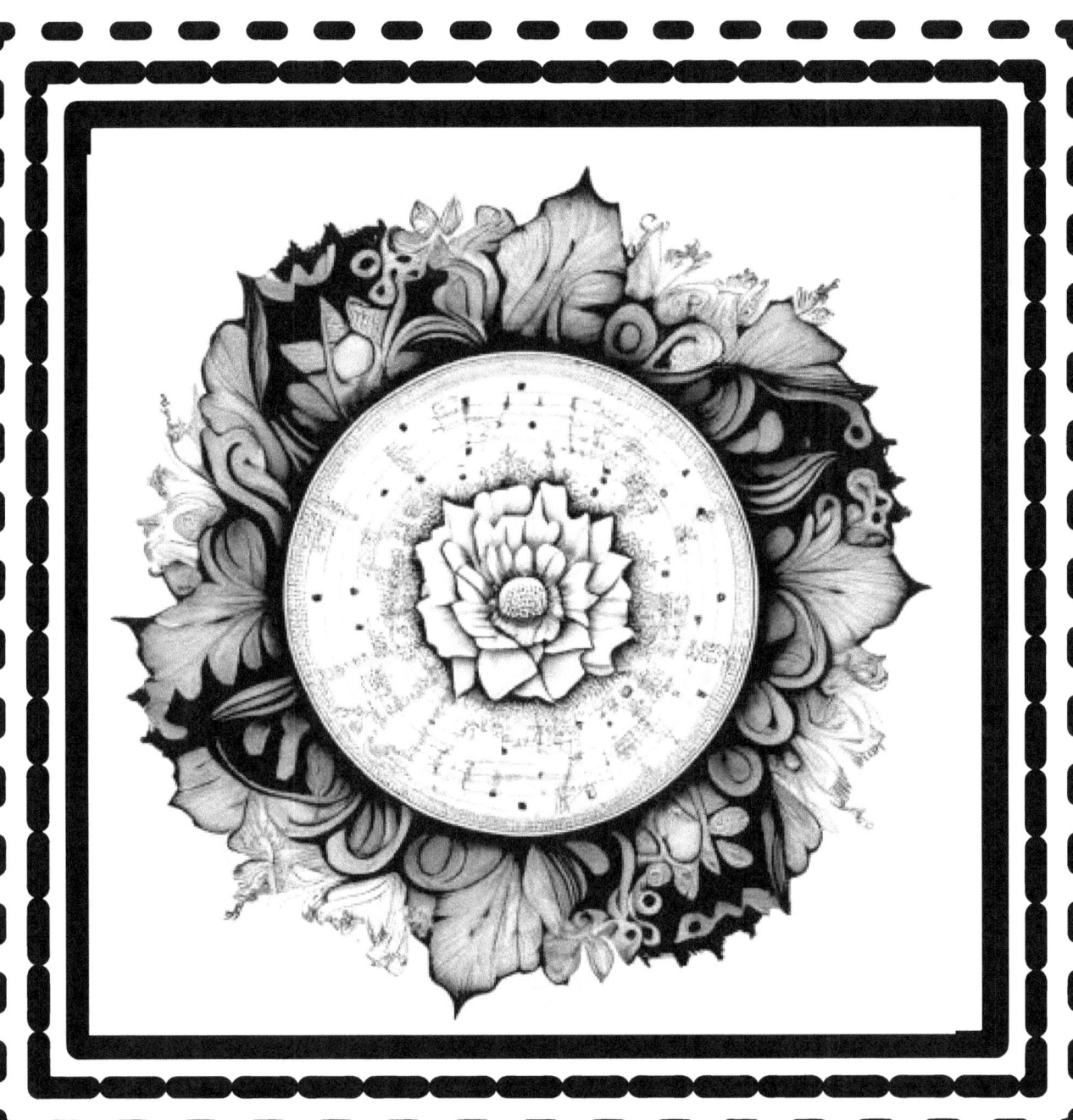

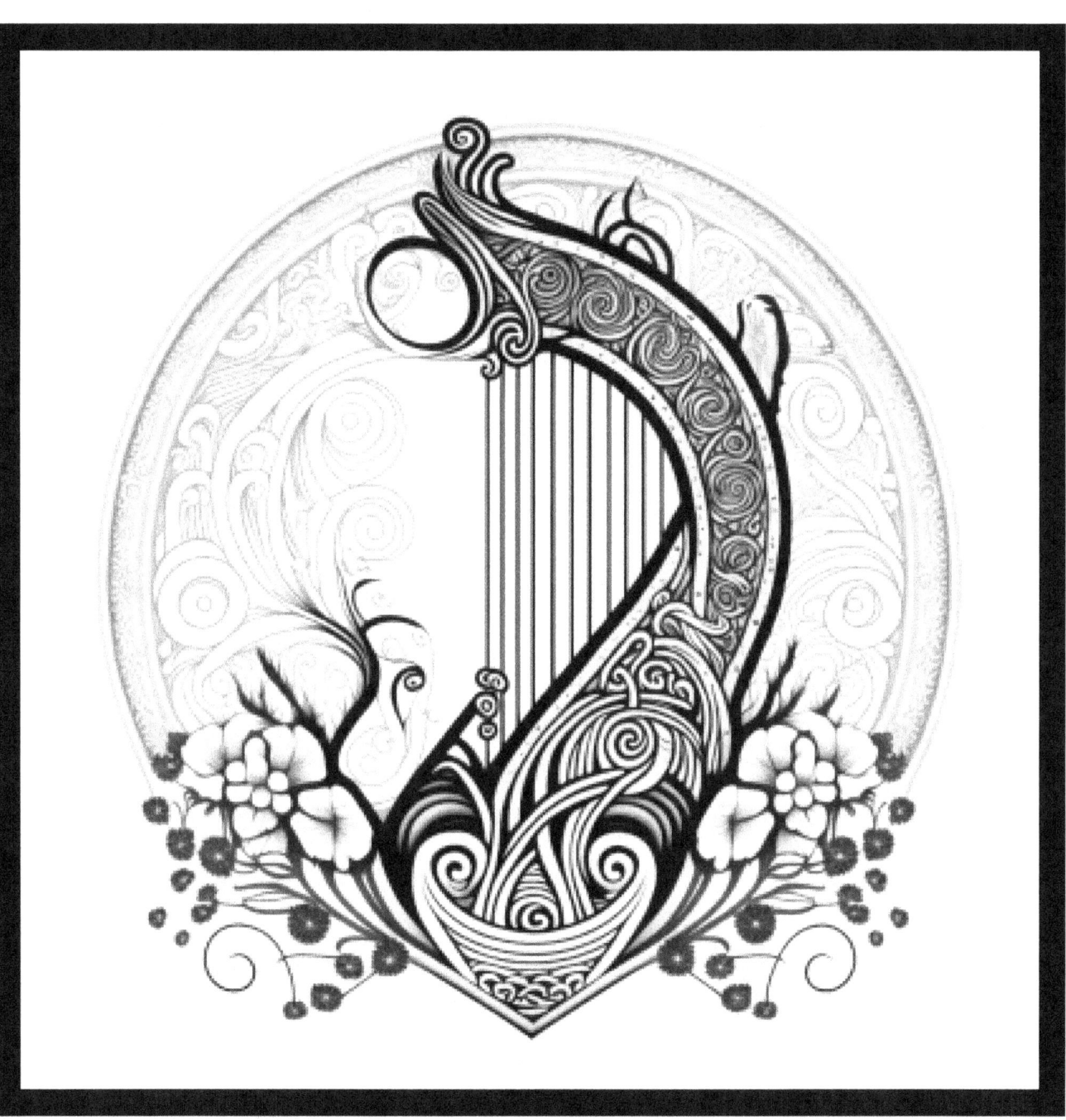

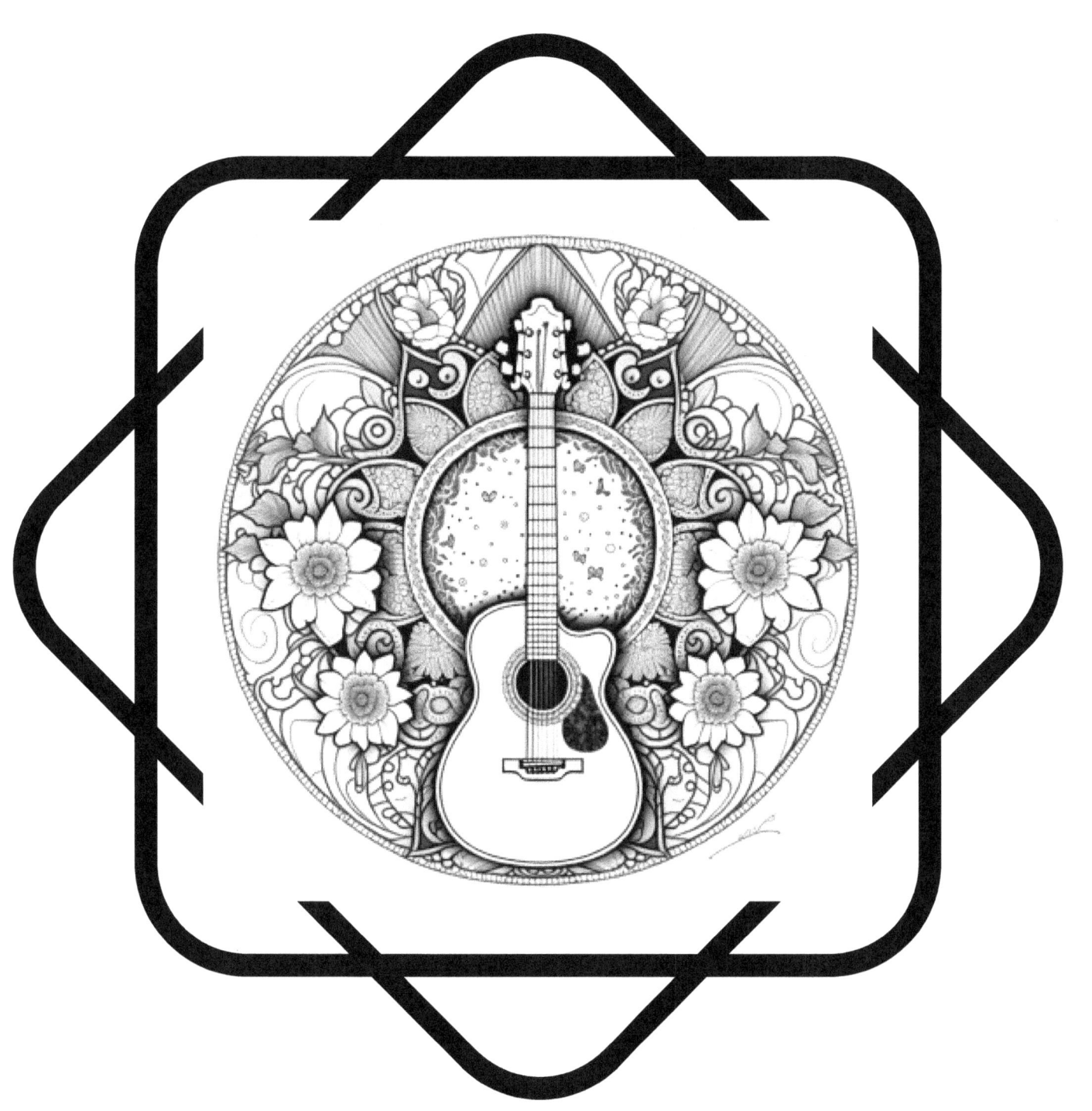

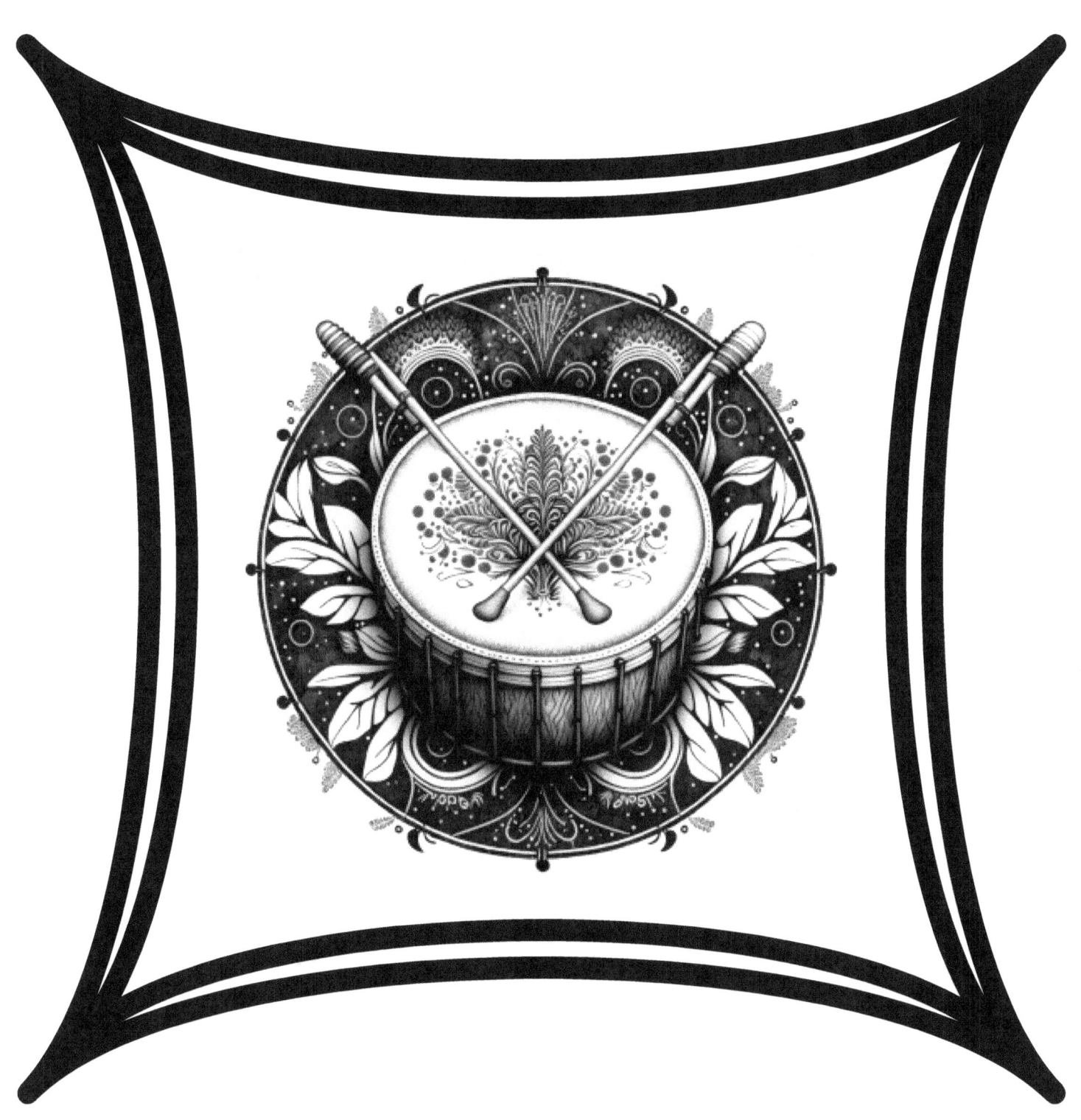

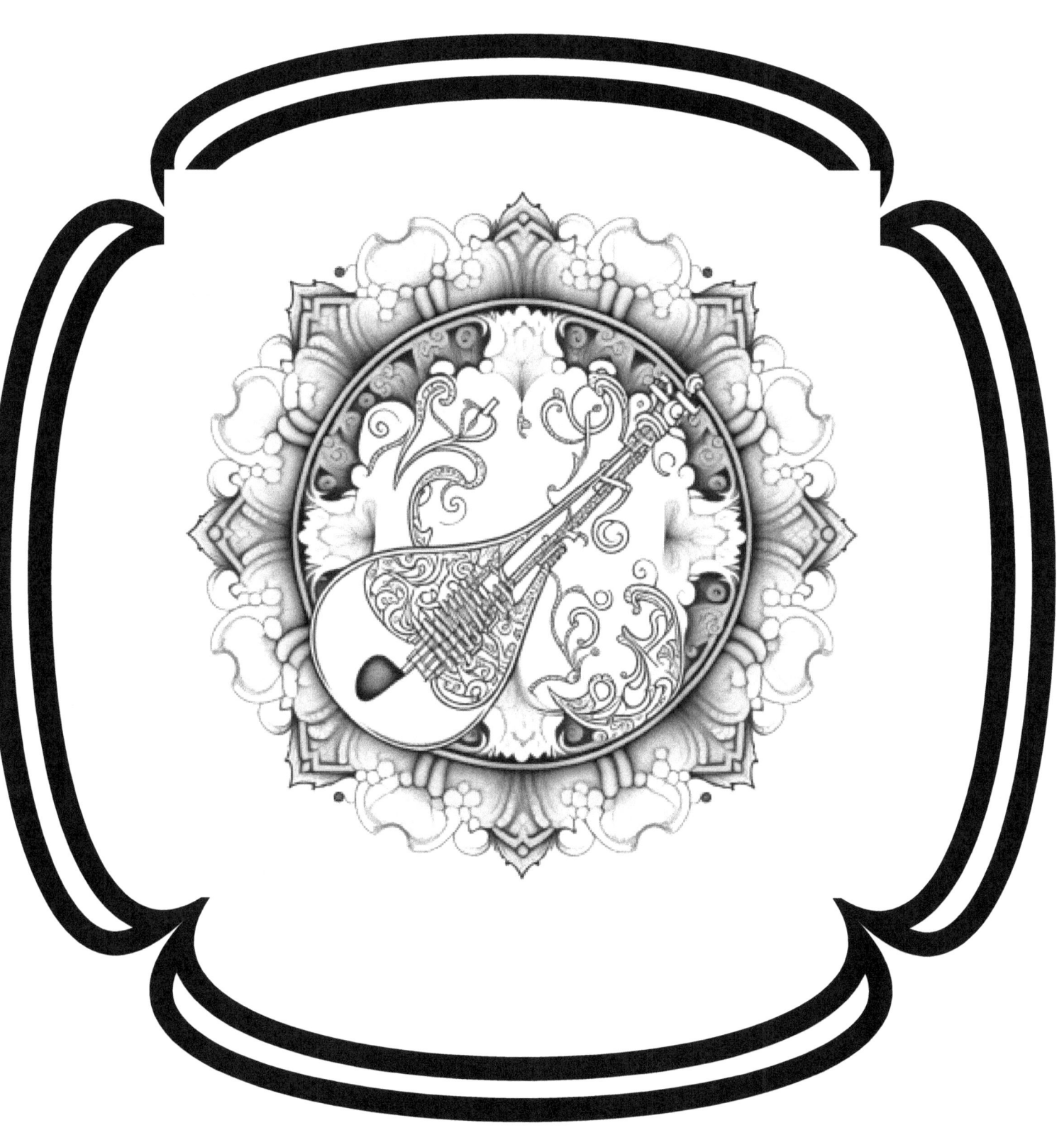

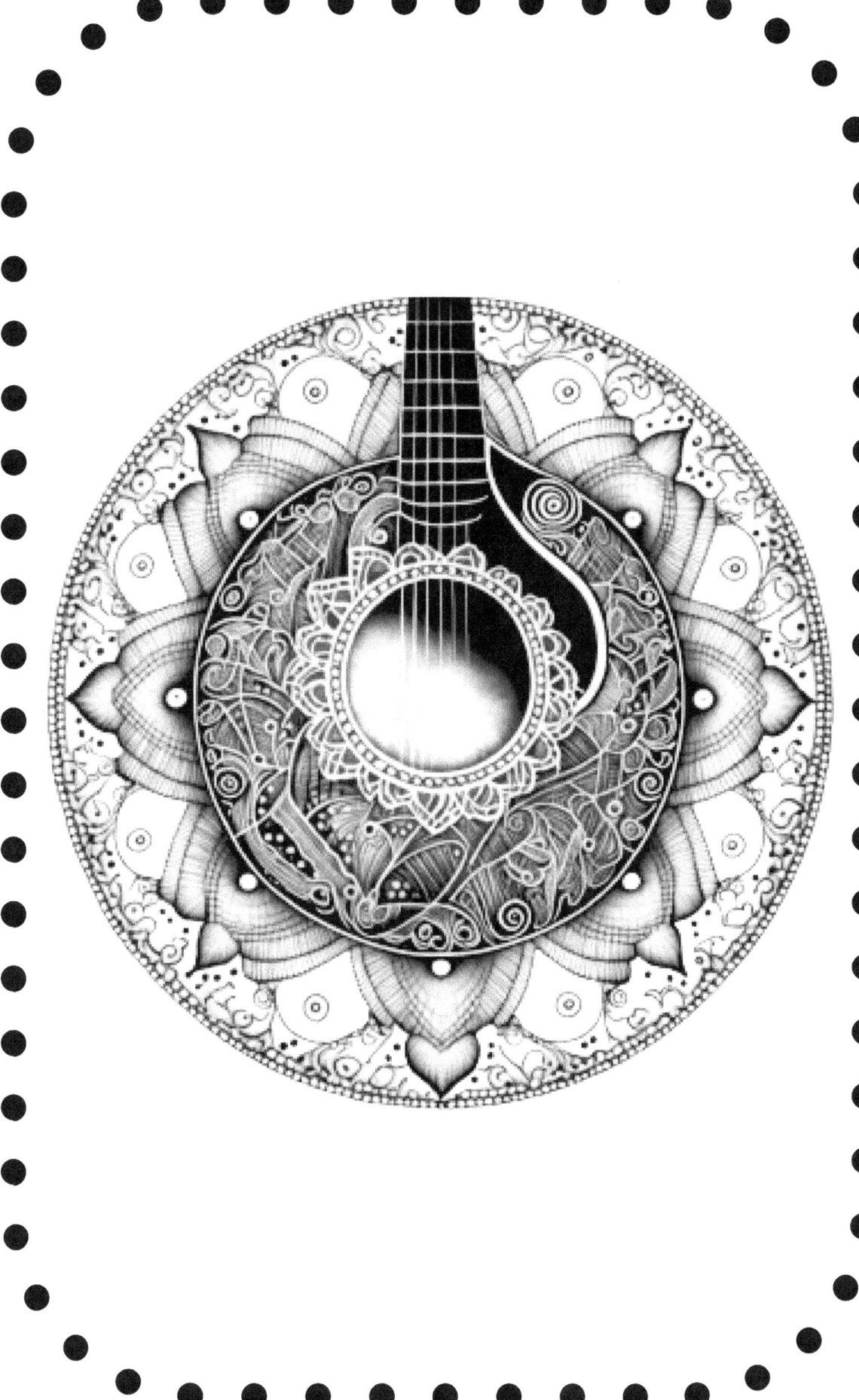

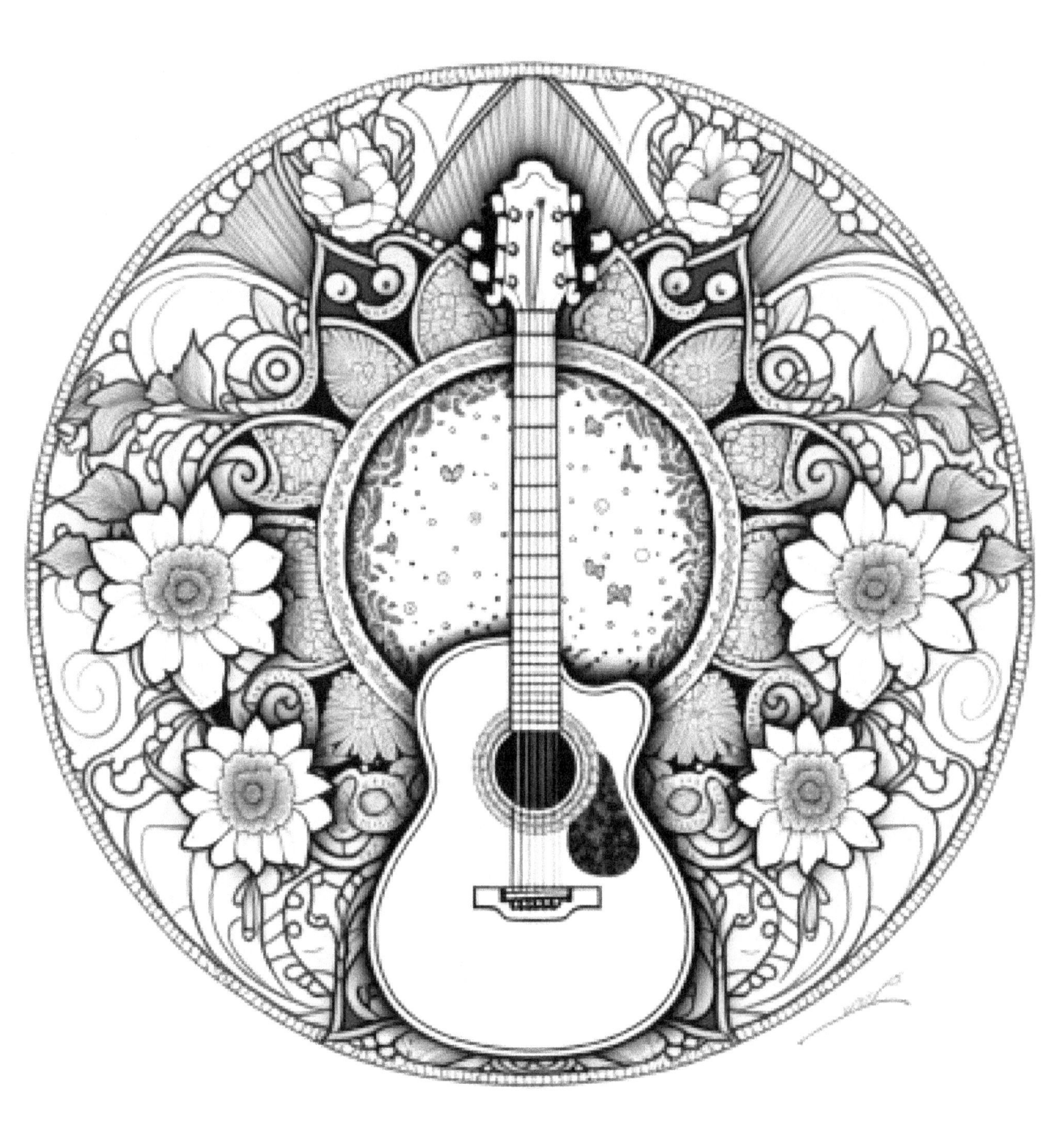

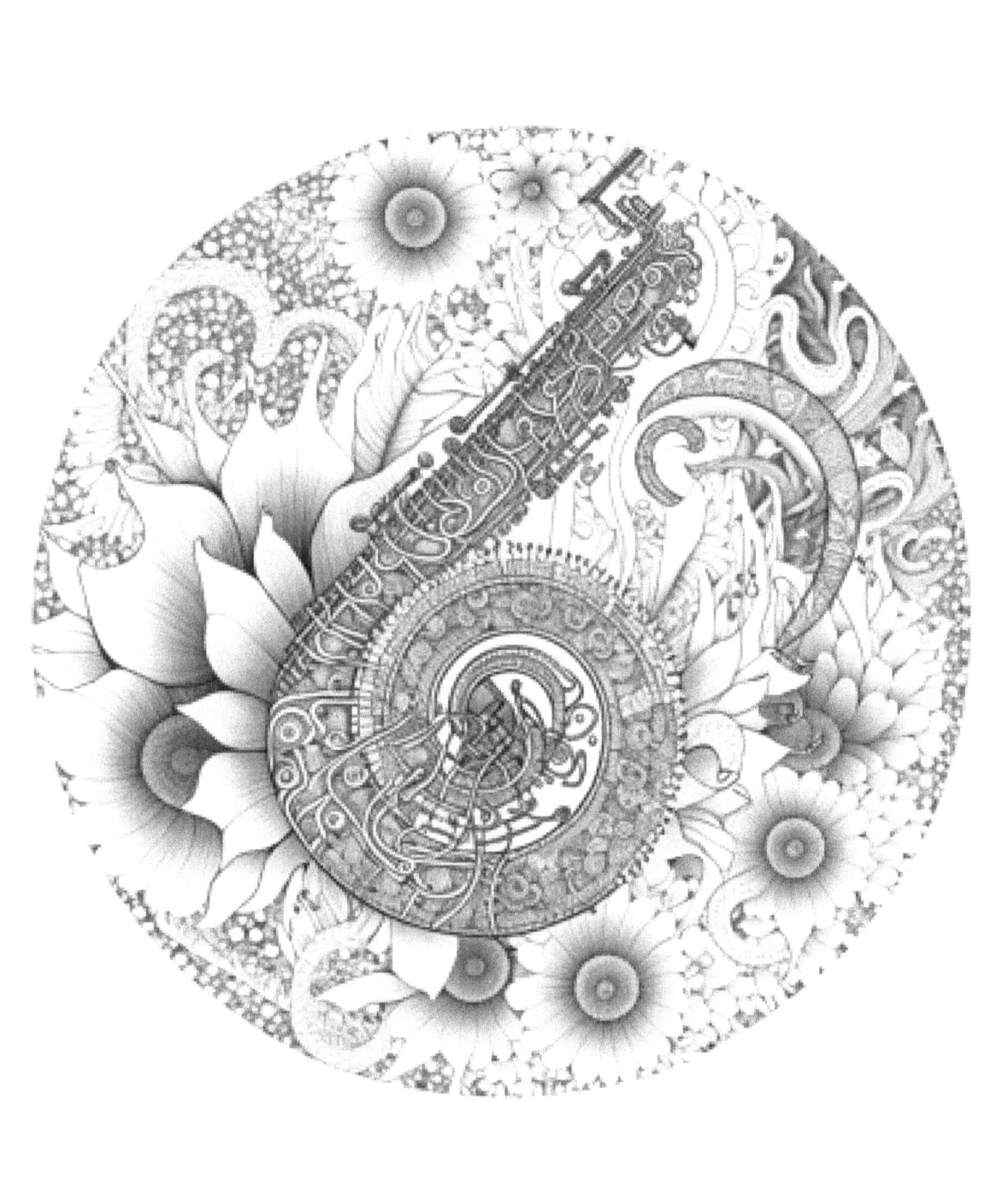

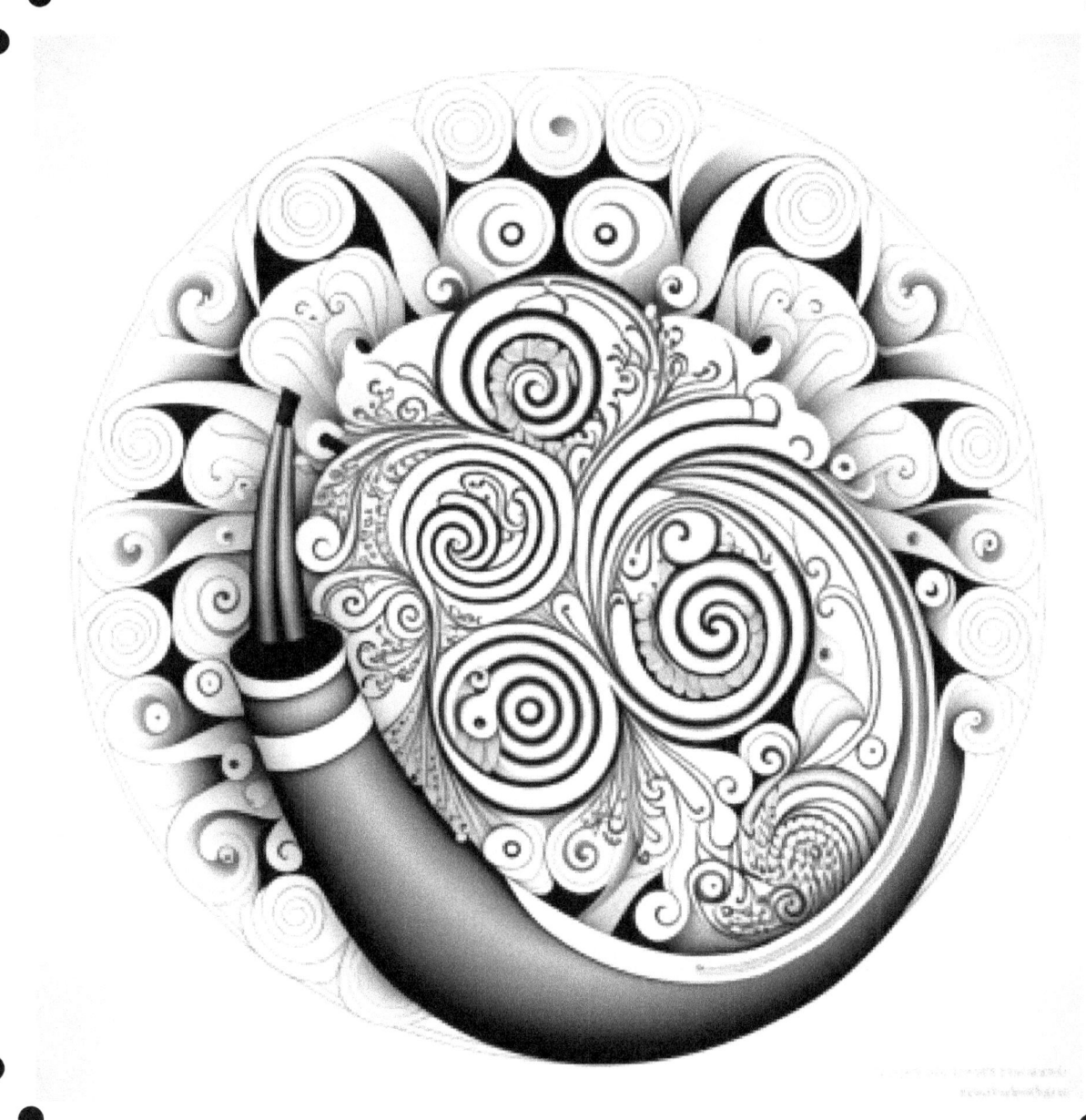

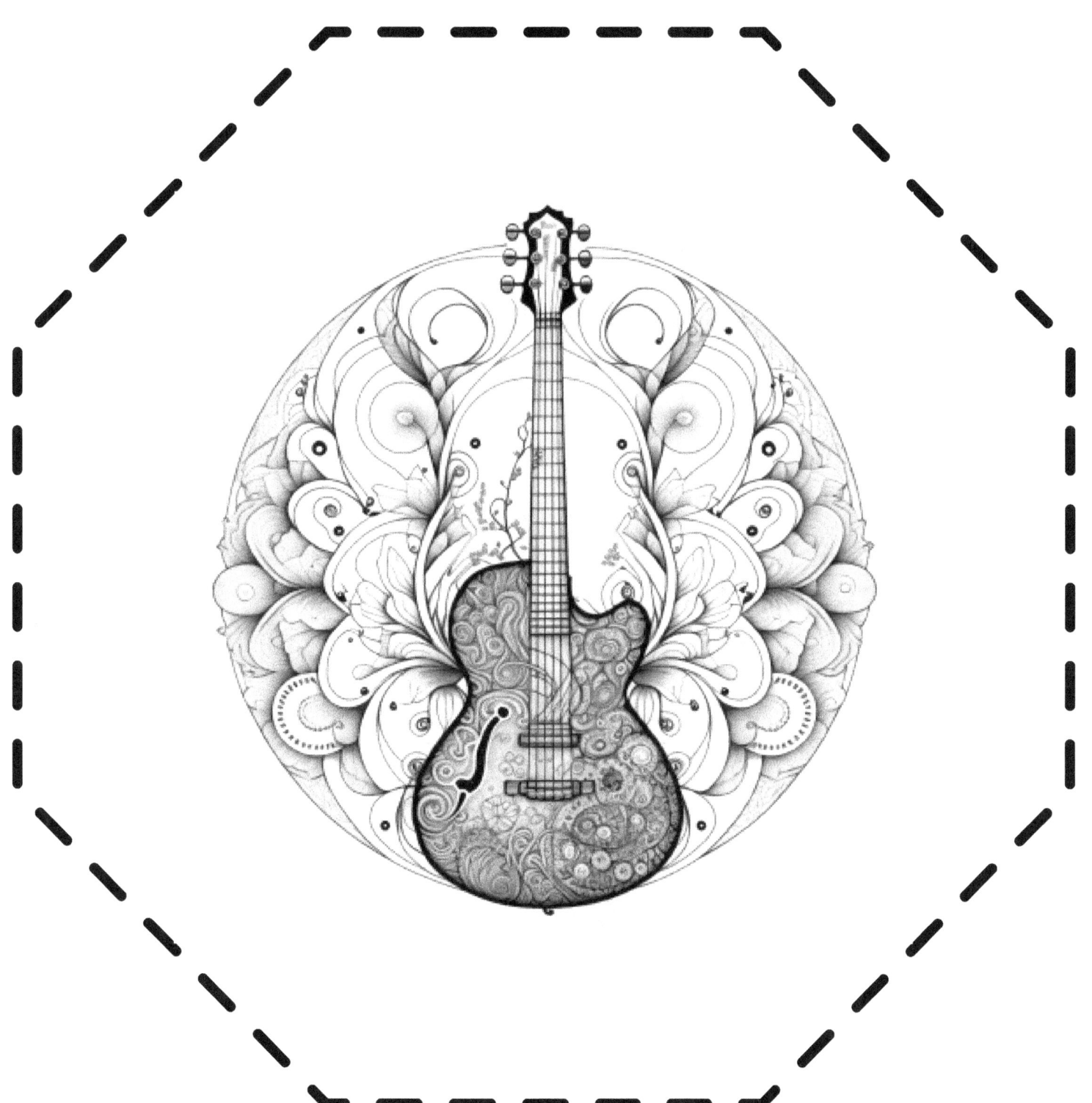

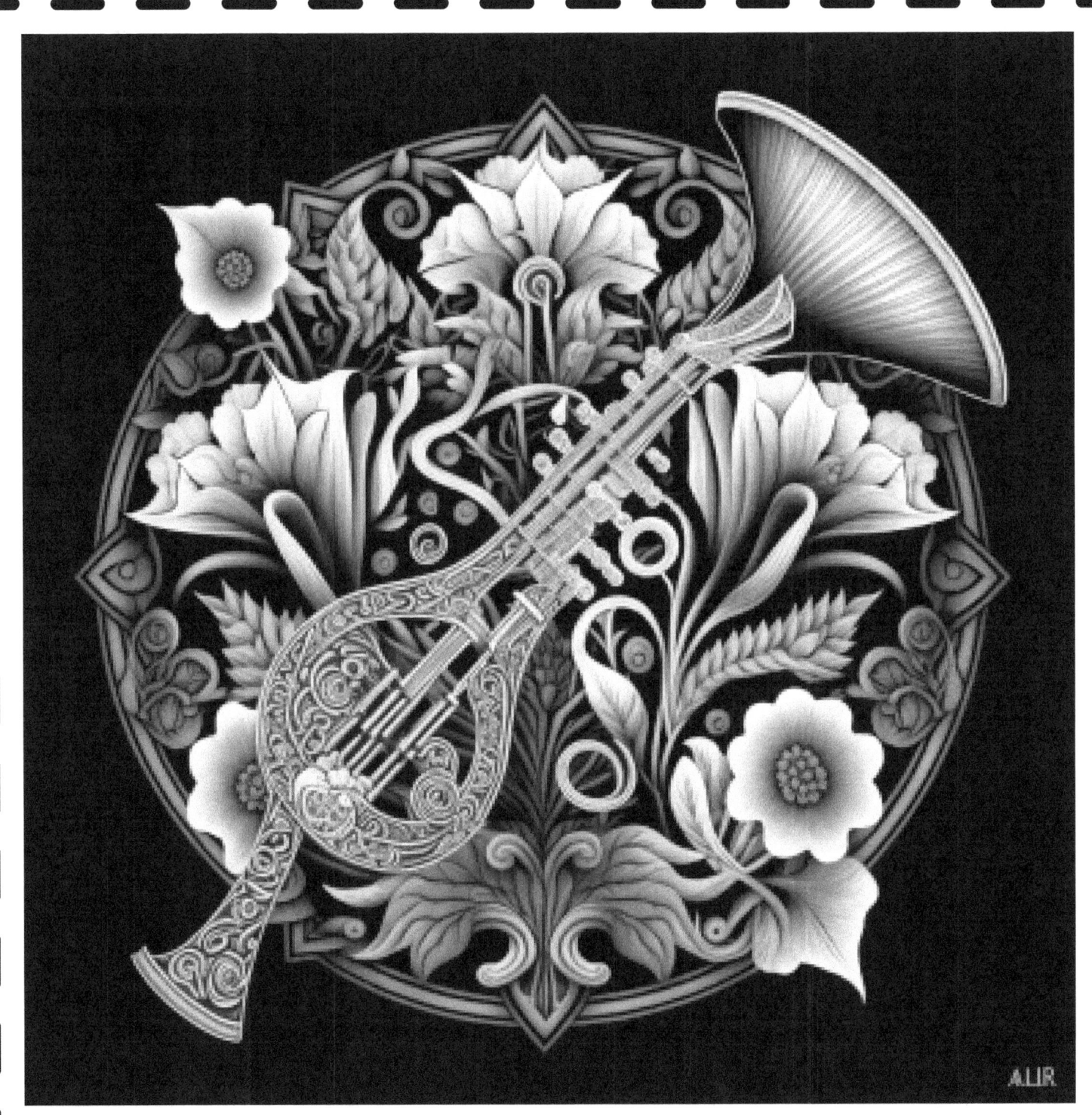

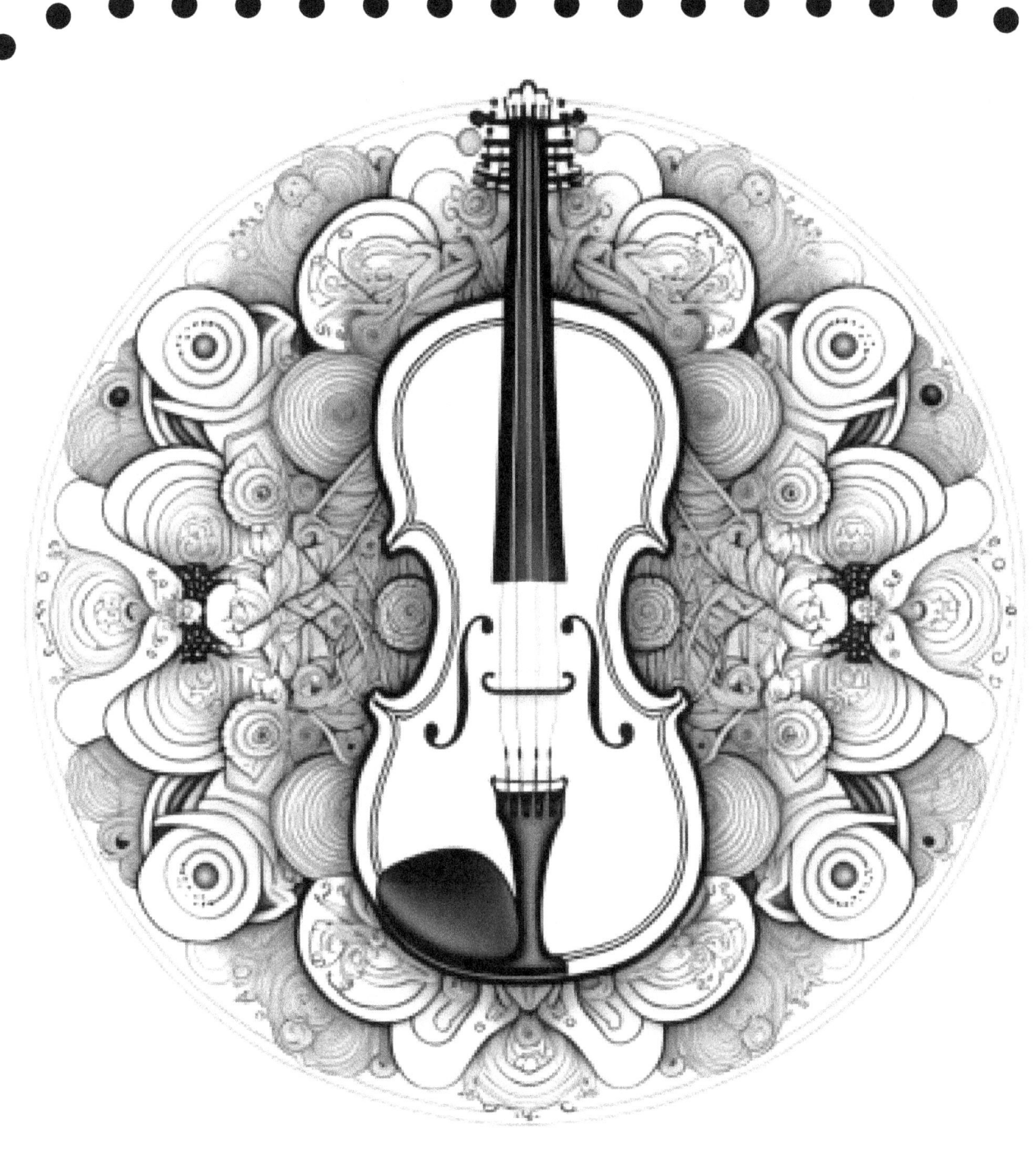

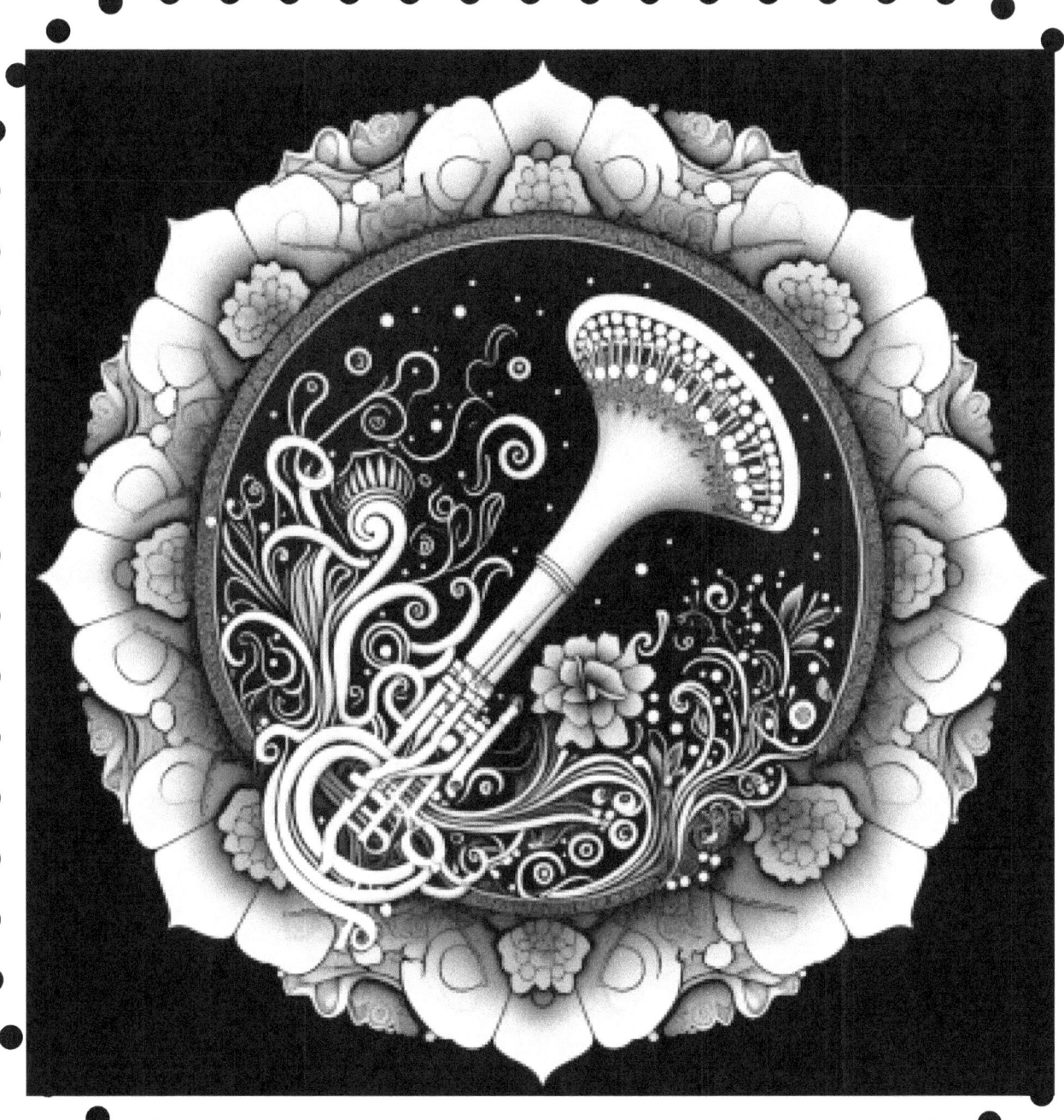

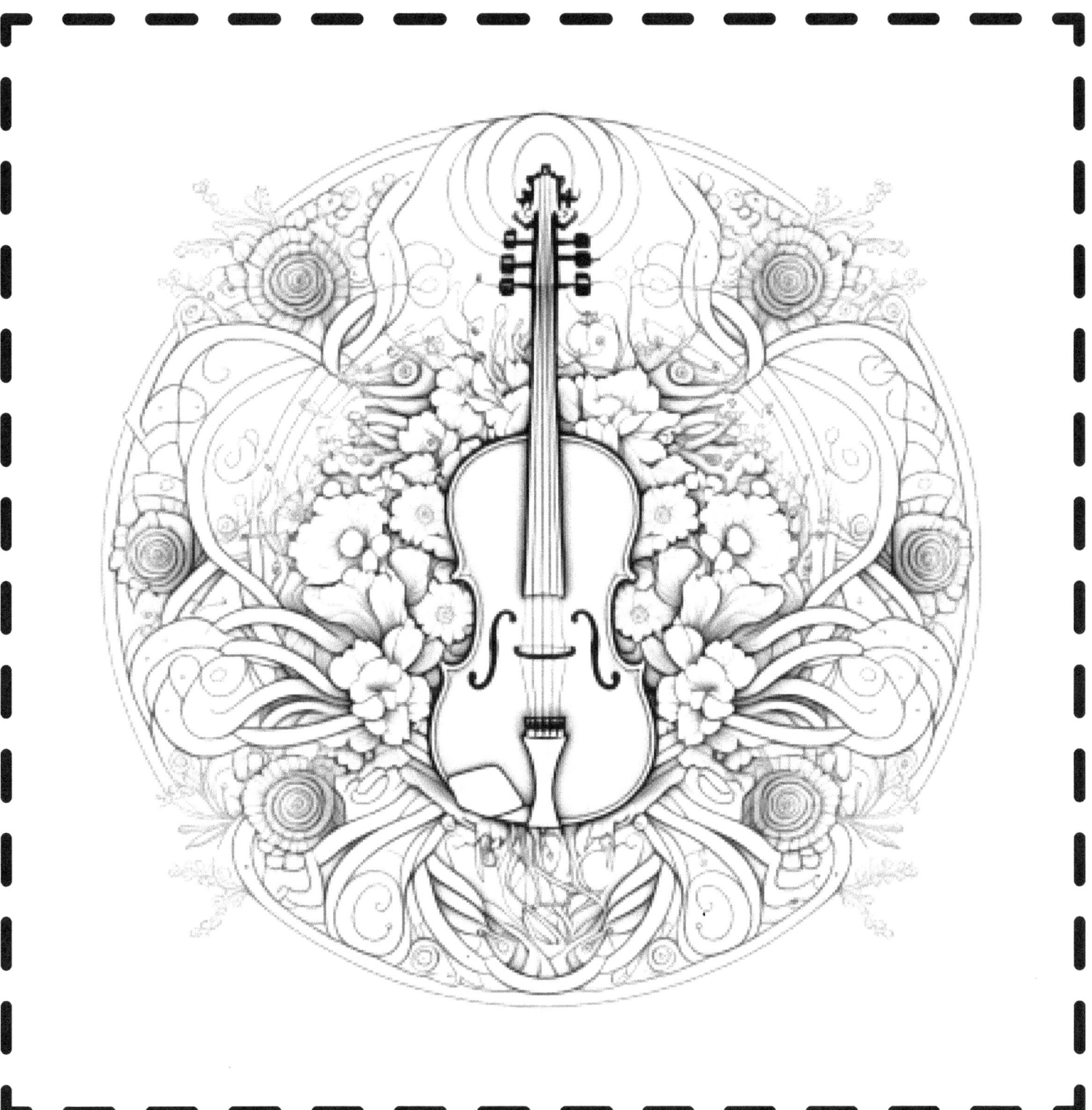

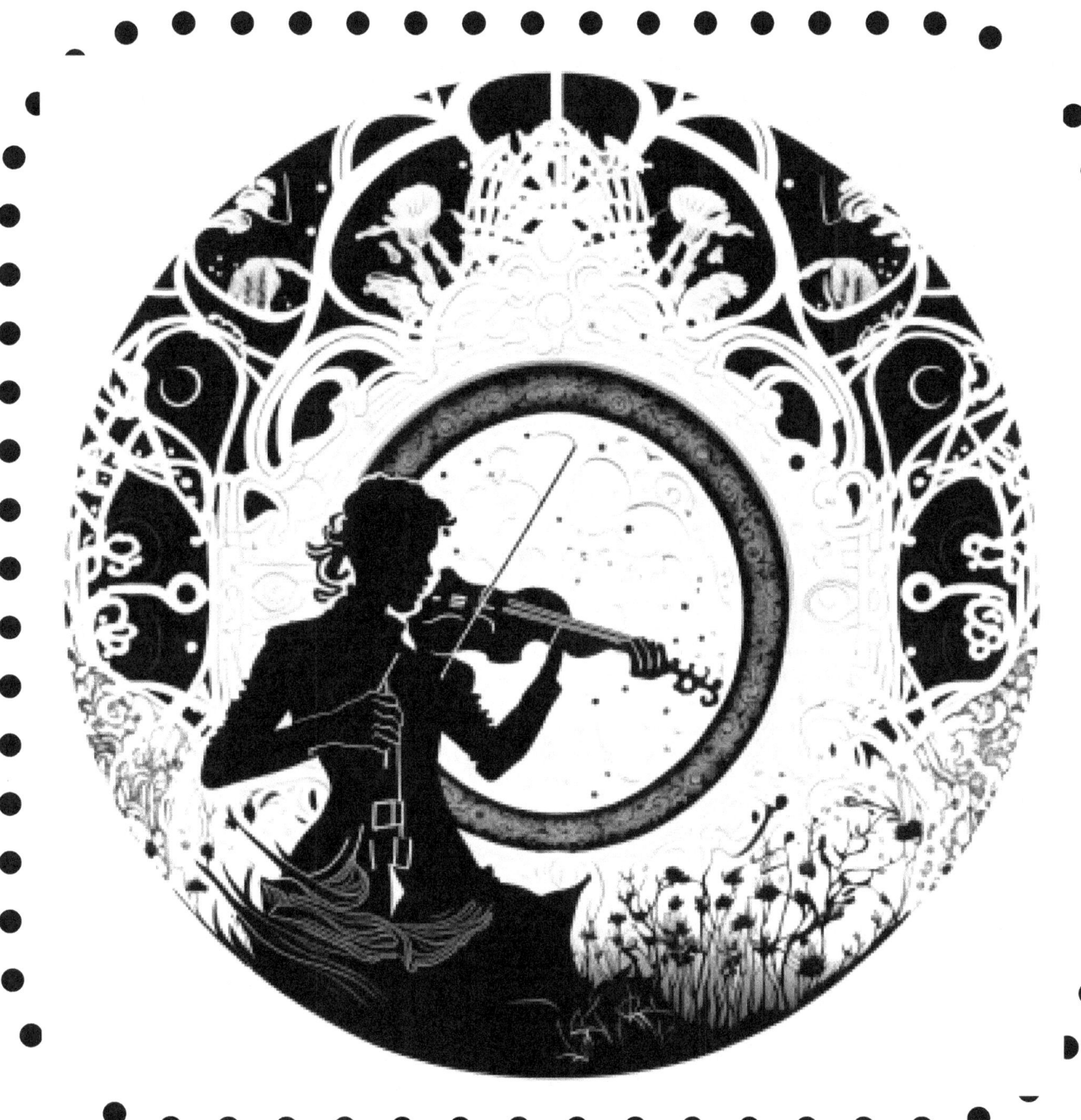

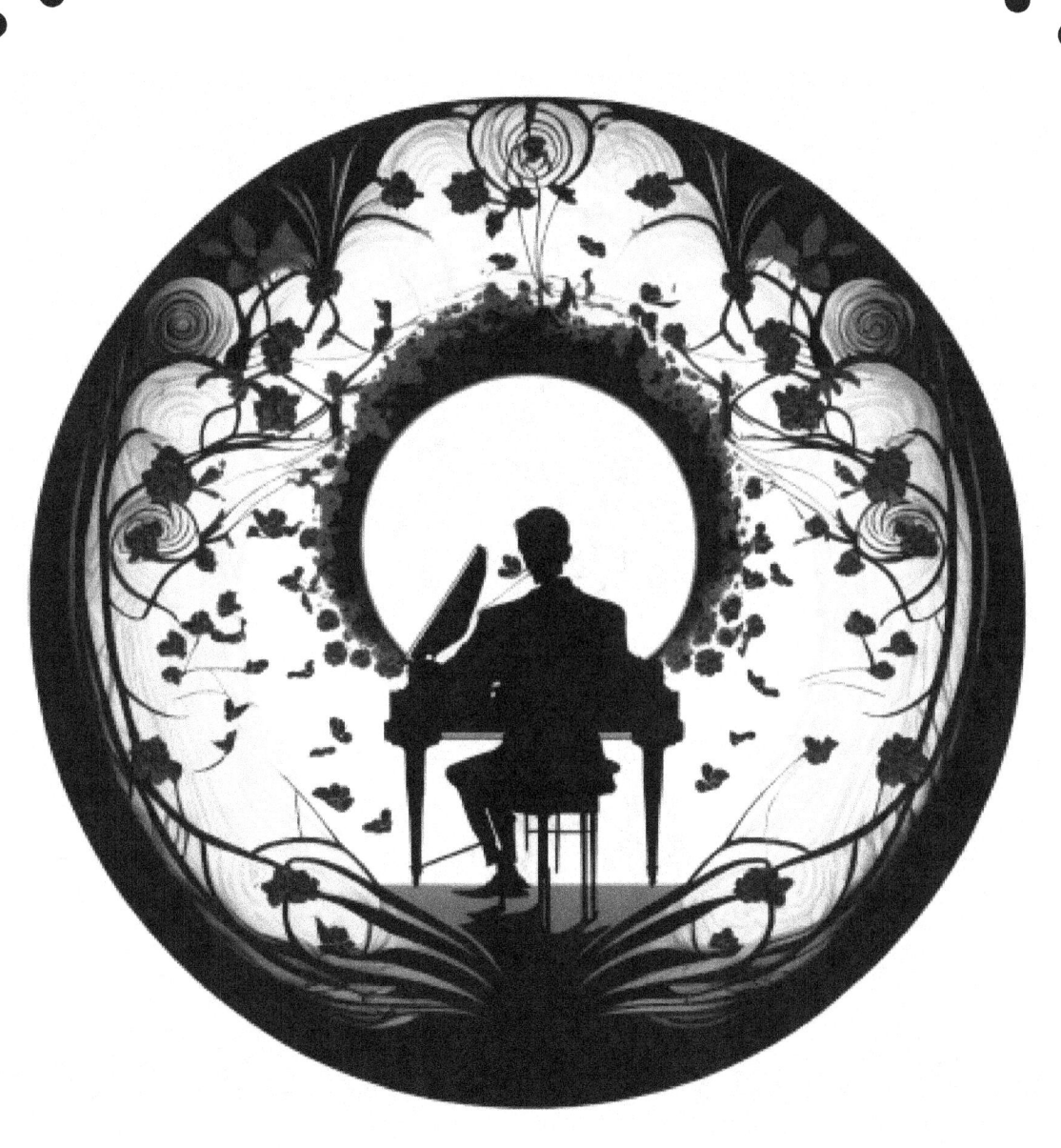

"BEING AT THE SHOW, WATCHING PEOPLE DO WHAT THEY DO SO WELL, HEARING A FULL ORCHESTRA, AND HEARING BEAUTIFUL MUSIC? THERE'S NOTHING BETTER."
COLIN DONNELL

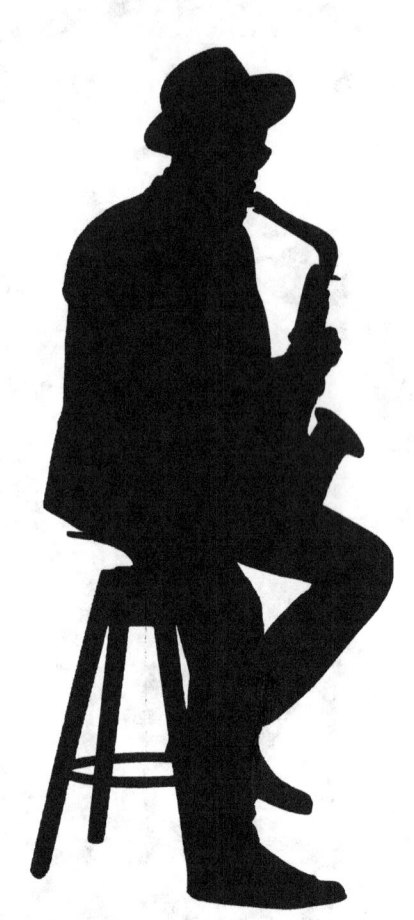

I THINK ANY TIME I'VE EVER GOT DOWN OR EVER FELT LOW THE ONE THING THAT PICKS ME UP FROM THAT IS WRITING A SONG ABOUT IT . AT LEAST YOU'VE GOT A POSITIVE EXPERIENCE OUT OF A BAD EXPERIENCE."
SINGER ED SHEERAN